Things Your **Father** Would Have Told **You**

Warren McDowell

WESTBOW
P R E S S®
A DIVISION OF THOMAS NELSON
& ZONDERVAN

WestBow Press books may be ordered through booksellers or by contacting:

WestBow Press
A Division of Thomas Nelson & Zondervan
1663 Liberty Drive
Bloomington, IN 47403
www.westbowpress.com
1 (866) 928-1240

ISBN: 978-1-9736-8657-6 (sc)
ISBN: 978-1-9736-8658-3 (e)

Library of Congress Control Number: 2020903099

Print information available on the last page.

WestBow Press rev. date: 6/25/2020

Contents

The key to happiness is getting stronger on the inside.

Pastor Alan Clayton, Ark Church, Conroe, TX

Dedication

To every young man, everywhere in the world - this book is dedicated to you finding your true purpose.

Dad, I know it's not your fault, but you died way too early. I still yearn to hear those words, "Son, I'm proud of you."

Son, you've given me so many challenges. I can truly say this book would not have been possible without your help. Don't be afraid to accept the responsibility of leadership: that's one of your gifts.

Your mother and I love you very much. You will only truly understand patience when you raise a teenager; therefore, be strong and courageous as you endure the storms of life. Each storm has its purpose as I've come to realize the things valued most are those that don't come easy.

Warren McDowell

Matthew 3:17 (NKJV)

And suddenly a voice came from heaven, saying, "This is my beloved Son, in whom I am well pleased".

Foreword by Pastor Robert Walker

God knows what it takes for young men to experience the satisfaction that comes from living a life of purpose—His purpose. In *Things your father would have told you*, young men will discover their God given purpose, through the heart of a father, that when applied will make a difference in all the key areas of their lives: their relationship with God and with family. The biblical perspective for money, success, and the legacy they will leave for their children.

If you put your faith in these words and are obedient to them, you will experience amazing things!

"I have written to you, young men, because you are strong, and the word of God abides in you, and you have overcome the wicked one." 1 John 2:14.

Robert Walker
Senior Pastor
The Prayer Room Church

Preface

It took a long time for me to realize the Principle of Sowing and Reaping. This book was written for young men who want to know the truth about becoming a man. The world keeps throwing sports, girls and alcohol at us as if these are the prizes to be won at all cost. Should we accept the media's image of us as mindless brutes always looking for a good time without a care but still wearing the best clothes, jewelry and underwear?

Who are you supposed to be? Is there a role model that you can follow? There are many strong women in your life but that's not who you are. What are the answers to being a man when examples of real men are scarce or just plain absent?

My dad worked two jobs and died before I got married. The many conversations we should have had never happened. I found myself shaping my version of a man on my own and it took a long time to learn how to be the man I was destined to become. Often, I felt alone in my search for the qualities of a true man. Not a worldly man, not today's man, not a changed man or even the once popular sensitive man. I wanted to be a real man.

Now a father, I want to give my son and young men all over the world the tools and lessons I've learned in a clear, concise dialogue that cuts through the junk we are fed daily. There are certain truths you need to know that will help you live. I've done my best to list the basic qualities that shape a man's values and character.

The advice in this book follows the Principle of Sowing and Reaping. Some say it's a universal principle, some say it's a natural principle, but I know it works because it's God's principle. The purpose of writing this book is to share experiences with someone younger in the hope they will gain knowledge, understanding and wisdom.

King Solomon asked the Lord for the ability to discern good from evil and He gave him wisdom. It is my earnest wish that wisdom is what you receive when you read it.

You reap what you sow son. Please start planting seeds now and grow in confidence knowing they will return with fruit watered by your reflection of God's love.

Acknowledgements

I'd like to thank all those who have supported me and responded to the call for help.

I'd like to express my sincere gratitude to my wife, who has always been there for me.

I'd like to thank my family, my friends who encouraged me and my two brothers who had the idea to write this book.

Lastly, I'd like to thank my son who through his life journey has inspired me to share what I have learned with the world.

Warren McDowell

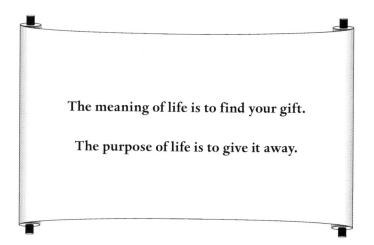

The meaning of life is to find your gift.

The purpose of life is to give it away.

This condensed version of a quote by David Viscott may answer one question yet it boldly asks another.

What is your gift?

Keep reading - between these pages there is an answer.

Let's begin

Warren McDowell

A guide for young men as they develop and mature

The elephant story

South Africa's wildlife parks have brought many animals back from the brink of extinction. They are also a tourist attraction success story. However, in the 1990's South Africa's parks discovered an amazing number of rhino deaths.

Poachers were thought to be the cause, but park game wardens soon discovered a threat never encountered before. The deaths were traced to the young male elephants. The elephants were introduced into the park as orphans and as they matured they became more aggressive. Young male elephants enter into, musth – a period of heightened testosterone, increased sexual activity and aggressiveness – before reaching manhood. Their aggression became focused on the next largest animal in the park – the rhino.

At first, the game wardens began to kill the young males in musth. Finally, older male elephants were introduced from another park, and not only did the rhino killings stop, but the young elephants experienced shorter musth periods.

1 Corinthians 13:11 (NKJV)

When I was a child, I spoke as a child, I understood as a child, I thought as a child; but when I became a man, I put away childish things.

Introduction

Who are you?

There is a time when you begin to ask for answers. Are you here by accident? Is there a divine plan? Why is the world the way it is? What's your place in it? When did this start? Where does it end? Who am I really? Who am I going to be? Should I care about anything else besides me?

You have numerous questions and some of them shout so loudly you just don't know how to put them to words.

You know you are here, stuck in your parent's relationship with the outside. They have created a private place with roles and responsibilities that they expect you to follow, but why?

Why should they expect you to blindly obey what they say when they don't even know you? They sink in yesterday's world while you swim in the present.

You search yourself and know for a fact that, that ain't right. They are always ordering you around. They tell you when to eat, when to sleep, what to do, what not to do, what to say and even how to say it. They think they know everything, but they don't even know you.

Problem is you don't know yourself.

The truth is there are a lot of questions that demand an answer.

Who am I	–	Identity
What am I	–	Talents
When am I	–	Potential
Where am I	–	Destiny
How am I	–	Origin
Why am I	–	Purpose

Life's experiences will help answer these questions, and finding the answers is what will help you become a man. This book is written to help you determine the part of your life you are living in – the when am I.

When am I forever removed from the label of boy and distinguished as an adult commonly known to the world as a "man?" To get from boy to man is different for everybody and takes longer for some than others, but there are certain stages we all go through as we grow. I call them the five steps of awareness. They are rebellion, anger, self-expression, self-awareness and acceptance. As we progress through the steps and shift our focus, we gain a better understanding of who we are.

Rebellion – Every male goes through a time when he rebels and begins to question everything and everybody. This is normal. It's the length of this period that presents danger. Rebellion never works and leads to the second stage.

Anger – There is only one direction to go when rebellion gets us in trouble and that is to get mad. We are angry we can't continue to be rebellious without suffering consequences.

Self-expression – Once we find we are limited on those things we control, we turn our creative energies to letting the world know how we feel through what we know that we can control, such as our bodies. This takes on a wide range of forms, from tattoos to art to music to sex. Our quest to express ourselves can be self-destructive if we are still locked in a rebellious cycle.

Self-Awareness – Eventually we learn what we do affects others. Though we may not verbally accept responsibility for those things that hurt others, we recognize our behavior has hurt people we care about, and we hopefully change.

Acceptance – The world is huge. There are few things you can readily change. The closest, easiest thing in this world to change is you. You start looking past the immediate and into the future. That's when you learn patience. Being patient comes with maturity. Once we know that the prize exists for those that plan to have it, we begin to take the steps to obtain the prize. That means playing by the rules. By this time, we know ourselves enough to have created our version of the rules. The rules are personal now. You know your limits and the things you need to do to get the things you want. Though you still focus on yourself, you recognize some things will not change and ADJUST. You begin to understand your role in determining your future. You start the journey by identifying where you were, where you are now and where you plan to be. As you change to meet the demands of the future, you travel the path to become a man when you do one important thing: *dedicate your life to a greater purpose.*

That's right a purpose greater than yourself. Some men do it when they embrace their passion – teachers loving to teach, fathers living for their children. Some never do it. Men take responsibility for their actions. Make this choice wisely, grow faithfully, trust God, become a man.

This book is divided into ten sections.

The 10 categories of MANhood

1) God is first
2) Family is second
3) Character is third
4) Passion is fourth
5) Goals are fifth
6) Money is sixth
7) Women are seventh
8) Hard work is eighth
9) Competition is ninth
10) Opportunity is Yours

Our Prayer for you

Ephesians 3:14-21 (NKJV)

[14] For this reason I bow my knees to the Father [l]of our Lord Jesus Christ,

¹⁵ from whom the whole family in heaven and earth is named,

¹⁶ that He would grant you, according to the riches of His glory, to be strengthened with might through His Spirit in the inner man,

¹⁷ that Christ may dwell in your hearts through faith; that you, being rooted and grounded in love,

¹⁸ may be able to comprehend with all the saints what *is* the width and length and depth and height—

¹⁹ to know the love of Christ which passes knowledge; that you may be filled with all the fullness of God.

²⁰ Now to Him who is able to do exceedingly abundantly above all that we ask or think, according to the power that works in us,

²¹ to Him *be* glory in the church by Christ Jesus to all generations, forever and ever. Amen.

It was on a small suburban football team that Adam found himself. Adam had played football for years; he was running back, receiver, safety and backup quarterback. Adam loved the game. He found out he loved to quarterback in the division playoffs after the starter was sacked three times.

That day Adam grew 12 inches in his heart, in his hopes and in his dreams. After leading the team to victory when his team trailed by 13, Adam had elevated his image to that of a tough, results-driven leader.

Adam was ready, not just to play quarterback, but to lead. His inner strength had grown wings, and he had to let it fly. Adam practiced every day that summer. He wanted to be ready for his junior year and lead his team to become state champions. He knew he couldn't do it alone, and he continuously prayed about being the best football player ever. He prayed for his team and most of all he prayed that he would be obedient to God's will.

At the start of the new school year, Adam and his teammates got the news of the new football coach. Coach Johnson had a mild heart attack and decided to retire early. Adam always knew that man shouted too much. He could think of all the times he said to himself, "Coach Johnson's gonna give himself a heart attack if he keeps shouting like that." Then

Adam switched gears to the new coach. Who would it be? Would they promote from within or would they choose a coach from outside the district, or even outside the state? Would he have to prove himself or had the new coach ever seen him play?

Coach Bloom and Wayne, a new student to the school, came about the same time. The first week of practice, Wayne began practicing as quarterback. After the second week, it became clear who the quarterback was going to be. Even though Adam and Wayne were evenly matched in throwing the football, the new coach favored Wayne. Rumors about Coach Bloom and Wayne being related didn't help.

Adam believed he was the logical choice and last year's record proved it? The night before the first game Adam randomly opened his Bible to Romans 8:28 – "And we know that in all things God works for the good of those who love him, who have been called according to his purpose." He knew that verse was speaking to his heart, and before bed, he hit his knees, proclaimed his love for his Lord and prayed that he would be able to play quarterback. He asked God to find favor in him, open his heart, make him wiser, stronger and a great quarterback. Adam felt calm after his prayer and went to sleep that night with a growing sense of peace and release. Whatever happens, Adam knew it would be for the best.

That Monday Coach Bloom called a meeting to announce his starters. Adam would be starting as running back, a position normally played by Brian. Adam was so disappointed and hurt he could hardly tolerate practice. That night he prayed for God's forgiveness, wisdom and strength. The next day he practiced like a galloping Great Dane and ran over everybody.

He followed that performance in the game to triple the score against the Eagles. Adam never liked running the ball before. In fact, he hated getting hit. He found that he was quick enough to fake out his defenders and create a hole large enough to run through. If he was going to run the ball, then he was going to make the defense work hard to catch him. His effort and determination paid off. Adam's running game was remarkable. He could dodge a hit better than a matador dodges the horns on a bull, but he still hated getting hit and ending up at the bottom of the pile. Every night he prayed to return to the position that ignited his soul: quarterback.

After the team's fourth win, Adam's prayer was answered. Wayne's father's job had shifted, and his family was being relocated again. Though Wayne and Adam were not the best of friends, they had talked enough for Adam to appreciate Wayne's winning attitude and ability to adapt to any situation. That's what helped Adam excel at the position of running back; understanding how flexible Wayne had to be to embrace the changing environments he encountered when his family moved. Because of Wayne's father's job, the family moved a lot which made Wayne tough. Before Wayne left, he confirmed that he and the coach were related. Rather than being upset, Adam was happy that he had developed a new tool in his quarterback talent tool chest. God had changed him on the inside, and now, before each game, he thanks God for strengthening, growing, listening and mostly loving him.

Putting God first confirms a promise for a long life by honoring your mother and father. Obeying the desire to lift your voice in praise when things don't go as you wish builds character. It takes humility to appreciate favor from God when you receive those things that surely you have not earned. Adam trusted God and revealed his heart. God blessed Adam and helped him grow. In the end, Adam emerged a better football player and person.

God wants to bless you. You should seek his plan for you here on earth but remember, this is not your home. As we prepare for eternity our lives are shaped, formed, readied and challenged to not only accept the gift of our Savior but to share that gift with others.

The best part is that you get to choose. You can humble yourself and accept a gift that will guarantee you a place in eternity. It begins by answering one question that will change your life forever. What do you think about the man named Jesus?

If you are unsure about Jesus, then Matthew, Mark, Luke and John give accounts of his life, death and life again in the New Testament. Why is this important? Because before you can truly satisfy the role of friend - husband - father you have to develop a relationship with Jesus. I've always marveled about the poem by Rudyard Kipling. I read it as a young man and loved the idea of being that type of man.

If by Rudyard Kipling

If you can keep your head when all about you
Are losing theirs and blaming it on you;
If you can trust yourself when all men doubt you,
But make allowance for their doubting too:
If you can wait and not be tired by waiting,
Or, being lied about, don't deal in lies,
Or being hated don't give way to hating,
And yet don't look too good, nor talk too wise;

If you can dream---and not make dreams your master;
If you can think---and not make thoughts your aim,
If you can meet with Triumph and Disaster
And treat those two impostors just the same:.
If you can bear to hear the truth you've spoken
Twisted by knaves to make a trap for fools,
Or watch the things you gave your life to, broken,
And stoop and build'em up with worn-out tools;

If you can make one heap of all your winnings
And risk it on one turn of pitch-and-toss,
And lose, and start again at your beginnings,
And never breathe a word about your loss:
If you can force your heart and nerve and sinew
To serve your turn long after they are gone,
And so hold on when there is nothing in you
Except the Will which says to them: "Hold on!"

If you can talk with crowds and keep your virtue,
Or walk with Kings---nor lose the common touch,
If neither foes nor loving friends can hurt you,

If all men count with you, but none too much:
If you can fill the unforgiving minute
With sixty seconds' worth of distance run,
Yours is the Earth and everything that's in it,
And---which is more---you'll be a Man, my son!

Great words, great deeds, great concept but the big question I always asked was HOW?

How do you stay that balanced? How do you harness your inner strength? How do you soothe the spirit, yet release the warrior within? "If" lets us know that there are countless challenges for us to bear. As we encounter each challenge our character is framed, integrity tested, our resolve is either strengthened or shaken. "If" begs us to believe our inner strength is strong enough to meet these trials. Is it? Can we develop the qualities it takes to be a man alone? Are we born with the will, strength and control it takes to conquer life's challenges? I don't think so. I believe we need help.

The only way to grow ourselves into even a faint resemblance of the man Rudyard describes is with God's help.

As Adam proclaimed his love and faith, he also held onto one of God's promises. You can too. Find a promise from God and hold on to it with your whole heart. I've found the one thing God cannot do – He cannot lie. His promises are true and His love everlasting.

Warren McDowell

Find out all you can about a man named Jesus. Pray for guidance, wisdom, strength, understanding, patience, and peace. Pray that you'll learn to love: the simple things you take for granted, others as much as you love yourself and yes even those that hate you. Be generous and always soften your heart to be able to forgive.

You can do anything, anything, when you put God first.

Even write a book? Yes, even write a book.

Find a promise from God, trust, pray, be blessed.

> Wisdom Tip
>
> Let Jesus be the one you impress

BOTTOM LINE – You need to have a relationship with Jesus. The more you know Him, the more He influences you to become a better man.

BLESSING - Luke 15:20 & 24(NKJV)

And he arose and came to his father. But when he was still a great way off, his father saw him and had compassion, and ran and fell on his neck and kissed him...For this my son was dead and is alive again; he was lost and is found. And they began to be merry.

A lanky, pimple-faced teenager with a big smile; John was 17. He liked attention, but wasn't getting much at the new school. John wasn't good at making friends. He just didn't seem to fit in. It wasn't until he told Oscar (a husky big-mouth senior) that his parents were going out of town the same weekend of Oscar's birthday that John somehow became instantly popular.

It didn't matter that John's twin sisters, age 13 and his responsibility to babysit would be home at this time. Lisa and Brittany, named after both parents' grandmothers had become official teenagers now that 12 was behind them. Physically, their bodies had changed and now half plums blossomed from their chests and hips were something they fought to have recognized.

Oscar is a user. He thinks everything and everybody owes him something. He uses a hug, smile and "Thank you, buddy" like the down payment for a car.

It took two weeks of constant nagging to get John to agree his house was the party place to be. Oscar was turning 18. He promised John girls, music, a small get-together with the right people and the guarantee everyone would help him clean up. Oscar promised he would steer the clean-up team and make sure everything was back in place with no evidence of anyone being there.

John bought it – hook, line and Oscar the stinker. He lied to his parents about being more than responsible for his sisters' safety, health and well-being. He said he understood the rules, that no visitors were allowed. Even when his father told him that this was a maturity test, John insisted they could trust him. After all, it was just one night. John's parents would leave early Saturday morning and be back Sunday eve. They left that morning thinking their son had accepted the challenge of caring for the house and those within it.

The festivities that Saturday night started early. Oscar brought all kinds of wine, beer and hard liquor. John thought it was overkill for such a small party and had warned his sisters to stay upstairs and play their own music. At 8:00 a small group arrived, at 9:00 more people and by 10:00 the house was packed. That's when things started going terribly wrong. A chair got broken and people were smoking everything everywhere. John knew this was getting out of control and went to find Oscar. After searching every room, John finally found him in the twins' room laying in the bed between them naked, passing a joint. John didn't know what to do. That's when the music stopped. The police were there and wanted to talk to the owner. John didn't mind. In his moment of desperation, anger and confusion, he felt relieved and ready to talk. First things first, he needed them to follow him to his sisters' bedroom.

Family carries various roles which though we may not choose are ours to bear. I cannot say enough about the special bond we create when we grow together as a family. We may argue and disagree but when it matters we know the needs of our family matters most. The roles you play are numerous, but the most important one is of obedience demonstrated faithfully by God's son. His role and yours are meant to glorify the Father. Your role as brother and friend prepares you for your future roles of husband and father. Being the oldest and the youngest son prove the most challenging. The oldest having to test parenting techniques first and the youngest growing with limited parenting when the schedule has become a routine. Being the only male child carries its own set of responsibilities. As John found out being responsible for others is not easy. You learn early the weight your presence commands especially in the area of security. This will not change so learn early and help your family as they look to you for your strength.

Your role as son to your mother and father may seem complicated but is clear and simple. As Exodus 20:12 commands it, "Honor your father and your mother, that your days may be long upon the land which the Lord your God is giving you". Honor means to hold in high respect. Regardless of how your parents preform in their responsibility of raising you, your responsibility toward them doesn't change.

My son, hear the instruction of thy father, and forsake not the law of thy mother: For they shall be an ornament of grace unto thy head, and chains about thy neck. Proverbs 1:8-9.

The way you treat your parents provides the foundation for your growth and long life. It would be foolish for me to say that young men always heed the advice of their parents. There will come a time when you believe you know everything. You think you are self-sufficient, self-dependent and invincible. No man is. This time passes usually followed by a leap in maturity. How long and harmful it becomes is different for every young man. The foolish seek fun and fortune; the wise seek wisdom. The challenge is when. When do you choose your future? Your heart will determine that. As long as it is filled only with yourself, you will be selfish and self-serving. When you open it to include others you gain an appreciation and understanding of true love.

As a friend you learn loyalty and trust, but the bonds of family transcend time. You experience the best and worst in a shared home where you are seen and heard every single day. Feelings are hurt, tempers flare and misunderstandings abound, but in these situations, you learn valuable lessons about forgiveness, trust and understanding. Friends change and so will your relationships with them. Some move away, others you ignore and there are those that you simply outgrow. Family members are forever. Healthy relationships with your extended family – uncles, aunts, cousins and grandparents – help you become well rounded and provide a wealth of experiences, ideas and opportunities. With older people, you will find the best way to receive respect is to give it. The respect you give others demonstrates your maturity. Grow, listen and learn from those around you.

When time comes for you look for a mate, you should know that women are the greatest survivors on Earth. The daily accomplishments they achieve are centered on the immediate. It is a man's responsibility to plan for the future. Before my wife and I were married, we sat down and wrote our "Rules of the Relationship." We promised never to argue in public. We agreed the last one out of the bed would make it up. We agreed that she would name the female children, and I would name the males. Our rules were focused on us and worked well. When that first heated argument began at a family event, we stopped and waited until we got home to discuss the disagreement. It wasn't until we had children that we realized we had no set plans to raise them, no agreed-upon idea of what we were doing, or what type of discipline we were using. By far our greatest arguments have been over how to discipline the children. The answers didn't come easy and the problems seemed to grow faster than our children. Our family unit seemed constantly under attack, and things didn't get better until I realized who was responsible for providing peace and understanding.

I was.

If you are fortunate to become a father, you will find the most precious gift God gives a man is his family. A father's role plays a very important part in a family's structure. Single-parent households in which the lone parent is the mother suffer when certain parts of the man's influence are never known. A dad's, "NO", has a different meaning than a mom's. My pastor once said, "A man is responsible for the physical, mental, emotional, and spiritual well-being of his family. Whether he knows it or not, he is the 'Spiritual head of the household.'" Father, lecturer, leader, disciplinarian, mediator, comforter, encourager, defender, pack mule, rule giver, police, security or peacekeeper; the roles of a father are too numerous to list. The example you set will forever live in the memories of your children. Their success depends on them following your example of love. Your success depends on you following your Father's greatest example of Love: His Son.

Embrace your role as son sincerely and remember wisdom comes from the Father. Open your heart to others, give respect and receive the same. In a friendship or with a potential wife communicate openly and honestly to create mutual understanding. There is no such thing as casual sex. There is a person that you can understand, encourage and share your life with. Even then there's a constant struggle to stay connected, keep the lines of communication open and learn to agree that you disagree. If or when your role changes to husband or father, you will be burdened with a host of responsibilities. Take the responsibility of planning a family seriously. Plan this step well for it is ultimately you who will be held accountable for your children's well-being. Not your parents, not their mother, not your wife – you.

If you provide safety, security and peace, you have gone a long way in helping your wife and children find theirs.

BOTTOM LINE – You are responsible for planning your family. If you are having sex, then you are planning on being a father.

BLESSING - Psalm 112:1-7 (NKJV)

Blessed *is* the man *who* fears the Lord, *Who* delights greatly in His commandments.

[2] His descendants will be mighty on earth; The generation of the upright will be blessed.

[3] Wealth and riches *will be* in his house, And his righteousness [b]endures forever.

[4] Unto the upright there arises light in the darkness; *He is* gracious, and full of compassion, and righteous.

[5] A good man deals graciously and lends; He will guide his affairs with discretion.

[6] Surely he will never be shaken; The righteous will be in everlasting remembrance.

[7] He will not be afraid of evil tidings; His heart is steadfast, trusting in the Lord.

There were six high school students sitting at the same table for lunch. One boy named Robert set his lunch and phone down then left to get dessert. As soon as he left another boy at the table, Anthony picked up the phone and stuck it in his pocket. He let the other kids know that if they said anything then there would be trouble. He then said he was going to the bathroom and left. Robert came back with a honey bun and started flipping out because he couldn't find his new phone. Susan told him Anthony had picked it up and was playing a joke on him. Anthony came back and said he didn't know anything about the phone. He even requested they search him and sure enough, there was no phone found on his person.

No one would back Susan up about seeing Anthony take the phone. Susan had to insist on what she saw three times. At one point she got frustrated because everyone looked at her as if she was the culprit. She just wanted everyone to know the truth. Having Anthony menacingly glare at her didn't help. They found the phone in another kid's locker, but the other kid claimed he didn't know how it got there. Later Anthony told Susan that he was going to "get her" for what she did.

Almost every day proves to be a test of your character. Whether you will pass depends on what you value. The truth is the most valuable possession you have. Never be afraid to use it. Susan told the truth even when threatened. When faced to make the hard decision which was also the correct one, she showed her friends what type of person she is. Later she asked each of them, "What if it was your phone?" Their response was a blank stare. It was clear what they valued most – nothing.

Robert is a starter on the football team. He told his teammates what happened and now Susan has a new set of friends. They told her that they let Anthony know things could happen to him if anything happened to Susan. Susan gained new friends, school-wide respect and support.

You can too, or can you? Can you be truthful in the face of possible harm or injury? Have you decided what means the most to you?

Who are you when no one's looking?

I used to love parties. I would arrive early and there have been times when the only person in the room before a party was me. The room was brilliantly set up with stunning tables and chairs professionally arranged. The tablecloths, center pieces, and candle lighting were perfect. As I inhaled the freshness of the moment, I couldn't help but dance. Lighthearted at first, then fast, crazy, sexy, Michael Jackson moon walking kind of sexy. Then I would notice that I was not alone.

Life gives you these moments and those that test you as well. What you think about yourself, how you treat others

Warren McDowell

and whether you keep your word provide the base from which your character stands. Be true to yourself. How can you like the man in the mirror when you can't bear to look at him?

There is a constant struggle to do what is right or do what is easy. This is a daily battle. Develop a passion for the truth and use it like Susan did. Like Susan you will find it's not easy, but honesty prevails when all else fails. Every day we struggle with half-truths, rumors, gossip and misinformation. It's hard to discern the truth, harder to avoid being part of the confusion. Now everything we see and hear gives us support to being selfish, self-absorbed and self-centered. How can we avoid the pothole of me? Those people lost in themselves share a common trait, they don't know who they are. They let their jobs define them. They let their family define them. They let their friends define them. When they are alone what they really feel is empty. It's the empty man that is easily swayed.

Think about what defines you. Currently you are about those things you value: God, family, friends, money, fame, relationships. It's easy to tell what you value the most and most people are so busy putting themselves first they don't have time for anything else. If you value relationships you will seek understanding, admiration then seek world acceptance, material things seek wealth, eternal life - Jesus acceptance and God's direction. What you value will help you set boundaries on those things you will and will not do. Do you need boundaries? Of course, you do. Some men will do anything for money. Some men will do anything for money provided no one gets hurt. Some men will do anything for money provided no one gets hurt and it's not illegal. These three objectives were set by one man. His experiences drove him to keep refining them to minimize negative consequences. Had he set his boundaries early, he would have avoided years of detention and frustration.

Becoming a man means you appreciate your values, know your boundaries and accept the consequences of your actions. You need to define who you are. Some men go all their lives being lost in Earth. As soon as you realize who you are: values, gifts, passion, purpose then you will be able to navigate the web of the world to your benefit. Guard your heart, seek wise counsel and never follow the advice or footsteps of a fool.

The way you treat strangers, co-workers and those you don't like is just as important as the way you treat your family, friends, and those you love. If you believe you are the most important person in the room, then you probably treat others like dirt. At no point in this world will you know everything. Being arrogant is just as harmful as being stupid. We all make mistakes. It takes a strong man to admit the mistakes he's made. It takes an even stronger man to apologize to those that were affected or hurt because of something he did. Giving an apology is not a sign of weakness. It is a sign that you are confident you know who you are; a human being with flaws and weaknesses as well as talents and strengths. It will also help mend the pain you caused others. As you learn to apologize, you should also learn how to forgive. Living with pain and hurt is a hard way to live. It can rob you of your happiness. As God forgives you, you should forgive others when they hurt you. As I live and breathe I can choose to be worried, mean and selfish or kind, loving and happy. I hope you choose the latter. It's much easier to live with a smile on your face than to go through life frowning and blaming others for your unhealthy attitude.

My mom always said, "Ain't nothing like a good understanding." If you give your word, then you have made a promise. Before legal contracts and binding agreements, there were men who made agreements by simply shaking hands. They gave their word they would live up to the agreed task. Living up to your word means, if you say you will do something, then do it. It's that simple. You will either be known as someone who can be trusted or not. Keeping a promise is a real test of character. No one respects or listens to a liar.

If you are making promises you can't keep, then you need to stop making promises. You need to realize only God cannot lie and base your actions upon the promises God made to us. Like honoring your mother and father promises a long life on earth or committing to the Lord whatever you do, and your plans will succeed. Understanding this fact helps solidify your character. It's up to you to act upon it.

You decide the rules to live by; whether you tell the truth, live up to your word and make good on your promises. That allows you to sleep well at night and have peace in the day. Choose to be an honest, fair, righteous man and you'll plant seeds of trust, justice and respect. A dishonest man will plant seeds of doubt, hate, scorn and distrust. His life is crowded in drama, confusion, jealousy, emptiness, then death. Choose truth, choose life and your life will be blessed with happiness. In the end you will win twice; here and in eternity.

> Wisdom Tip
>
> Truth is always a friend
> to an honest mistake

BOTTOM LINE – If you truly want to enjoy your life – fill it with honesty, respect and love. Remember the great battle of good versus evil is waged daily on the inside. Ask for God's help, surrender to His will and become a conqueror.

BLESSING – Philippians 4:6-8 (NKJV)

[6] Be anxious for nothing, but in everything by prayer and supplication, with thanksgiving, let your requests be made known to God; [7] and the peace of God, which surpasses all understanding, will guard your hearts and minds through Christ Jesus. [8] Finally, brethren, whatever things are true, whatever things *are* noble, whatever things *are* just, whatever things *are* pure, whatever things *are* lovely, whatever things *are* of good report, if *there is* any virtue and if *there is* anything praiseworthy— meditate on these things.

"It don't get any better than that," James would say right before he asked for the sale. James was what you call a born salesman. He knew what, where, how and when to push to create that magic moment that ends in an exchange that can only be described by the word: Sold. James could compliment, cajole, and convince almost anybody on his way of thinking.

Being a senior now, he had his teachers fooled and was having the best senior year ever. That's because one year ago James quit working for the Men's clothing chain and started working for himself. At 16 James was becoming one of the best at Handsome, a major player in men's fashion. James realized he had a talent and passion about selling at an early age. It started with school fundraisers, then candy and gum in school.

As a freshman, it was baseball cards, concert tickets, anything that had a high profit margin and low inventory. At Handsome, James embraced his passion and sold suits to all that walked in, but that was his starting point. He sold ties, handkerchiefs, belts, shoes, socks and shirts. If there was a barber in the store James could have sold haircuts to make the customer's handsome image complete. James realized he didn't sell a product, he sold dreams. The thrill of the sale became his passion, but James wanted more. He wanted a lot more money and he wanted to get it doing less.

James bought his first ounce of weed at age 17 and he was able to triple his investment. He liked that. It wasn't long before he was buying two pounds at a time. Then he found cocaine to be lighter and the recreational drug of choice. Selling it was easy. He turned his next-door neighbor Alice, a beautiful, inquisitive, freckle faced redhead onto cocaine just to get her to kiss him. He saw she had a fascination with escaping the present and getting lost in the world of false happiness and contentment. He became her supplier, but James was surprised at how fast the effects wore off and she yearned for more. He had to cut her off, especially when she flipped out and threatened to tell his parents, the school, the world. James was done with her. What James didn't know was Alice's parents were going through the beginnings of a divorce and escape was what she was looking for.

James was now at Tre's house, a few blocks from his own where Tre and Ricky wanted to celebrate Tre's pre 18th birthday. They asked James for an 8 ball (one-eighth of an ounce of cocaine.) Since Tre had the house for himself that night, they planned to party all night. They said they were going to pick up a girl to have fun with. James knew about the prostitutes on Main Street and warned the boys about the dangers of unprotected sex with them. He stayed to have a beer with Tre as Ricky made a run to the store. James felt like sharing and told Tre the story of his first female sexual encounter. He was just about to leave when

Warren McDowell

Ricky came back with a girl in the car. James felt somewhat embarrassed and quickly composed himself to leave. Ricky came in shouting, "Got a girl in the car and she is good to go." James just shook his head and walked to his car. As he started the engine and shifted into reverse he noticed the flowing red hair. He peered through his window and knew for certain, it was Alice.

No amount of money could have prepared James for the feelings he had now: astonishment, disbelief, guilt. He shrugged his shoulders, gritted his teeth and vowed to do something different with his life and gift of selling. He knew that day his choices has led someone to sell their body, their presence and possibly their soul.

Each of us is different. As we discover ourselves, our relationship with the world changes. Just as we develop our talents we need to recognize our weaknesses and not take advantage of the weaknesses in others.

You are special – a one-of-a-kind creation. You are born with certain gifts that set you apart from anyone else. Your unique abilities are buried within. Maybe you were doing something, and someone asked you, "Hey, how did you do that so fast" and you said, "It was easy." Maybe for you it was easy, but not for everybody. Some of us discover our gifts early and some late, or we may use part of our gift and never experience the joy of it being fully known. You need to know. You need to find your strengths and develop your gifts. Take the time to try new things and don't be afraid of failure. After all, knowing your strengths, weaknesses, likes, dislikes and those things you enjoy the most will give you a clue to the real things you are passionate about: singing, talking, writing, managing, creating, changing, finding, saving, recycling, painting, teaching, pasturing, building, always growing. You will grow and prosper when you align your gifts with God's will.

Only you know the things that move your soul. Those things that gladden the heart are rooted in love. Your passion is the drive that moves you to act beyond reason and gives you general happiness. It's putting all of you into what you do because you love to. You need to know what pushes you toward perfection, grow that love and not be afraid to learn to lead with it. You should begin by asking yourself, "What is it I love to do?" What you'll discover will help unbind the chains that strangle your potential. It will also help you release the man you are meant to be.

Grow the love. Once you discover your love, love it back by giving it the time and resources it needs to grow. One way waste is defined is called unrealized potential. A lot of men carry that burden with them, and you can tell something is missing. The greatest gift you can give yourself is to be a whole man. When you grow your passion, you release your potential and increase your chances of reaching your destiny. Part of growing into manhood is making the decision to trust your gut, your heart, your love. This is the key to unlocking your true potential; taking the chance to dare the unknown by challenging yourself to be the best in those things you love.

Be true to yourself and use your passion to help others. As James found out, using his gift for his own selfish reasons can hurt others. Following your passion and aligning with God's plan will carry you past the worldly traps that snare the confused. Knowing who you are helps you find your passion. Knowing your passion helps you push past mediocrity to achieve a greatness you never thought possible. Now here's the thing. God gave you several gifts, talents and/or abilities. When you use these to glorify Him, there is but one word to describe the path you blaze through this world – unstoppable.

Learning is a lifelong journey. Delight in its path and seek wisdom from God. When you know yourself enough to use your talents and follow your passion you are on your way to achieving your destiny. All knowledge in the world is nothing without our Father's direction. Use your talents and passion to glorify Him and elevate your place in eternity.

No matter what, your true success will be measured in how much you give back. Give generously, your passion and the strength of your character will determine how successful you are doing the things you love to earn a living.

Wisdom Tip

Time stops when you're
doing the things you love.

BOTTOM LINE – Find your passion, dream big dreams, ask for God's help and you will overcome the world.

BLESSING - Psalm 37:4-5 (NKJV)

[4]Delight yourself also in the Lord,
And He shall give you the desires of your heart.

[5]Commit[a] your way to the Lord,
Trust also in Him,
And He shall bring *it* to pass.

Goals are fifth — *Philippians 3:12-14*

Wayne went to three different high schools. He got bounced from place to place and finally ended up staying with his grandmother. Wayne didn't like school and because he was older, he felt he didn't fit in.

When someone asked him what he wanted to do with his life, he said he didn't know, or he just wanted to live it. He dropped out of school, but his grandmother convinced him to go to night school. He didn't like that either. Finally, he got a chance to go to a special school for high risks youths. It was a mentor program run by ex-military that promised to turn his life around and guaranteed him a GED, free college entrance exams and a shot at several scholarships if he would stick to it. After 3 months Wayne was fed up and quit the program, or as he would say, the program quit him.

Wayne went back to living with his grandmother. When he took her car out late one Saturday night, he got involved in a high-speed chase. Going 90 mph around a corner, he lost control of the car and hit a concrete barrier. Wayne died instantly and left his friends remembering his words about what he wanted to do with his life, "I just want to live it."

Do you know where you're headed? Can you set short-term, mid-term and long-term goals and still be able to surrender yourself to God's will?

Having goals isn't about doing what you want in a certain time for your benefit. It's about humbling yourself, seeking God's will and enabling yourself for victory. As Roman General Maximus Decimus Meridius declares in the movie *Gladiator*, "What we do in life echoes in eternity."

Life is short. Living your life in the now doesn't prepare you for eternity. What matters most is the, "Why." Why are you here?

During my own search for self, I realized that to truly gain my life, I had to give it back. My goals became less self-centered, and I started planting seeds of generosity. When I passed a man or woman in the street with a sign asking for money, I would stop, ask God if it is His will to move my heart to give and He would give me an answer. I began to trust in that answer. I found I could talk to God, ask His help and receive a blessing when I aligned my goal with God's will.

My wife and I built a house, that is we took on the role of General Contractor, interviewed the sub- contractors, hired the ones we liked and paid them when the work was inspected. Although we told them their work would need to be inspected before we could pay them, they always insisted on getting paid after the work was done. Our goal to finish the house did materialize after seven stressful months.

Each step of the way we encountered various challenges, that with much prayer we were able to overcome. The main challenge was getting everyone finished the day

Warren McDowell

before inspection. Our house was built in five stages from a construction loan. An itemized construction build list served as a checklist to receive the corresponding five equal amounts of the construction loan.

The more parts completed the more we were entitled to receive. The same point went with the less complete the less of the loan amount we would receive. Imagine what happened when I would tell a contractor I couldn't pay them until the next inspection cycle because his job was incomplete.

Believe me they had workers to pay and none of them were happy when things weren't finished on time. Despite the immediate tension we were able to stay on time and on task. We (my wife and I) had to overcome the obstacles and avoid the distractions. In addition to the obstacles that get in your way the next biggest point of failure are distractions.

There will always be people, places, parties or other projects that try to elevate themselves in your priority list. It's very easy to put off what needs to be done today until tomorrow. Distractions are goal killers. As you mature you'll learn how to avoid then. Experience comes with time. For now only single-minded determination will take you past the potholes waiting to seduce your time.

We finished the house in seven months. We had it inspected three different times and know for sure the foundation, framing, plumbing, electrical, roofing, painting and appliance installations are sound. The secret to our success is simple.

We prayed. We had 3 house framers to choose from. We prayed that the wrong ones would be taken away and their cell phones quit working. One of the contractors finished early and just had to be paid before inspection. We prayed and another told us he would bill us with a 15-day invoice enabling us to meet the urgent need and stay on budget.

Whatever your goal, it's best to have a partner. Write your goals down, the steps it takes to get there and the time you plan to finish each step. Put in celebration moments where you reward yourself for completing that step and lastly don't start another goal project before you finish the one you're on now.

Wisdom Tip

Don't take your eyes
off the finish line

BOTTOM LINE – Visualize your goal, stay focused and you'll learn how to overcome obstacles. Remember, the most important part of achieving your goal is having one.

BLESSING – Proverbs 3:5-6 (NKJV)

Trust in the LORD with all your heart, and lean not on your own understanding; in all your ways acknowledge Him, and He shall direct your paths.

Michael's next-door neighbor had a very big front and back yard. Michael arranged to cut the yard with two friends, two lawnmowers and a Weed Eater. The boys worked hard Saturday, cutting and edging. One of Michael's friends, Pete, had never cut a yard before. Consequently, the area Pete cut had to be re-cut to get the grass he missed and smooth out the uneven parts. Wayne did a great job at edging while Pete was using the lawn mower. Mr. Dave had asked the boys to pay special attention to his sprinkler heads but Pete would run right over them. They started and finished late.

Afterward, Wayne had to go home and Pete spent the night. The next day Michael and Pete went to see Mr. Dave. He told them about the parts done well and not so well, then he reached into his pocket to pay them. He said since there were 3 boys, he was going to give them $30.00. Pete was so excited when he saw Mr. Dave pull out a 10- and 20-dollar bill that he snatched the 20 and immediately left. Michael had to apologize for his friend. He knew the way Pete acted probably meant he'd never get a chance to cut Mr. Dave's yard again and this was the beginning of summer.

When Michael finally caught up with Pete, Pete insisted that since Wayne was not there to collect, he shouldn't get paid. Pete also said that he should get the whole 20 since he did most of the work. Michael blew up. After the fight, Pete called his mom to pick him up. He said Michael was no longer his friend and he wanted none of the yard cutting money. Michael, however, gave $10.00 to Pete's mom.

Both boys learned a hard lesson that day.

Before you start a business venture with someone, determine the important things first. What needs to be done, who will do what based on their experience, what determines the job is complete, who will collect the payment and lastly how the money will be distributed. From simple to complex corporations today, all operate with simple rules that determine and distribute profit.

YOU NEED TO MAKE YOUR OWN MONEY

Men need to work. You need to do something that generates income. If you think dad, mom, uncle, grandmother or even the woman you are staying with will continue to give you money and let you live for free, then you have a life-lesson to learn. Do the things that displease those who are providing money to you, and that lesson will be taught early. When others are in charge of your money, then they are in charge of you. You need to earn your own money. The satisfaction of accomplishment alone will boost your self-confidence.

Money follows passion and goals because if you seek your passion and decide to be the best at something, then the money will follow. Often, we get caught up seeking the financial rewards and end up doing something we hate for the rest of our lives just to provide for our family.

Warren McDowell

Discovering what you are good at is important. Letting your interest drive your income is challenging. The reward of a long and successful career in an area you love is scarce. Typically, people experience mid-life crises when they realize they are stuck. You don't have to go down that road. Although you may not know what you are good at now, your job is to figure that out. Do enough different things to push yourself. Find and know your strengths and weaknesses. Educate yourself to strengthen both. Then when you realize your passion and talents, take a chance on them, knowing that your goal is to be the best at what you do. Your expertise will eventually land you the income you desire. Do it step by step, one goal accomplished at a time. Focus on personal development and professional growth. If possible, find a mentor in your field to work with.

Let your passion drive your goals; let your goals drive your income; let your income build your wealth. Manage your money wisely.

First, Give back to God.

Second, pay yourself and avoid the credit traps by having a savings and an emergency fund.

Third, create a budget and use the "save to buy" method instead of the world's "borrow to buy" way. Providing a home is the single biggest expense for you and/or your family. That cost should never exceed one-third your monthly take-home pay.

Overall, I like the 10-10-80 rule for managing your money: Give 10%, Save 10%, Live on 80%.

That's give 10 percent of your income, save 10 percent of your income, then live off the 80 percent left. The 10 percent giving will increase your happiness; whether it's to your church or charities. The 10 percent savings includes the emergency fund which after growth will allow you to decrease your insurance payments by increasing the deductible knowing you have that amount at hand. Living on 80 percent ensures you are a lender and not a borrower.

When you are in debt, you are a slave to the lender. When you are ready to buy a home avoid financial products like Adjustable Rate Mortgages (ARMS), Interest Only, Balloon or Jumbo mortgages. Go with a traditional 15- or 30-year fixed loan. A fixed loan may not sound as attractive as the others, but you can be assured it will not change. You can adjust your spending, stay on budget and stick to it. You want to definitely know where your money is going.

Lending money to a friend has ended many a friendship. If a friend needs money, gift them what you can spare. If it is not enough, then they can borrow the rest from someone else. Leave your gift and friendship intact.

When dining out, leave a generous tip. Remember tipping is as much a part of the budget as dinner is. Using credit for meals and entertainment is never a good idea. Always use the disposable cash at hand. Lastly, purchase big ticket items with cash. Go for the thrill of the hunt, and then make your kill with less of the asking price. Sharpen your

Warren McDowell

negotiating skills. If something costs $500.00, offer $450.00 cash now. Ask to talk to a manager, take the money out and let them know you are serious. Let them know you are on a budget and this is what you have allotted for this purchase. Mention you wonder what their competition would do if you offered cash. If you get good at negotiating, then you'll only have to save up 80 to 90 percent of the cash before you go on your hunt. Take your ready cash and use your negotiating skills to seal the deal.

> Wisdom Tip
>
> Money never comes from worry

BOTTOM LINE –

Honor God – give to church and charities

Pay yourself – save a percentage to establish an emergency and savings fund.

Don't be a slave to debt – stick to a budget and pay with cash.

BLESSING - Jeremiah 29:11 (NKJV)

For I know the thoughts that I think toward you, says the Lord, thoughts of peace and not of evil, to give you a future and a hope.

At the ripe age of 16, Dan knew he was a big baller. He had worked the summer and had a savings account. His parents were proud, and they decided this year for the Thanksgiving holiday to go on a cruise instead of visiting relatives.

Dan didn't care. Getting out the house – even with his parents and older sister – was to him an escape from the day-to-day dullness of just existing. He just didn't let his parents know he welcomed the change.

The cabin on the cruise ship was so small it was claustrophobic and worse than that, he had to share space with his sister. Dan thought this was going to be the worst vacation ever until he met Emily, who just happened to go to the same high school as he did. Dan's sister, Wanda, met her first. Emily is a senior, but as they met up that week to dine, shop, play games and just hang out, she became a close friend. Dan didn't know anyone as sweet, honest or beautiful as Emily. Wednesday, Wanda chose to sleep in and Dan spent the entire day with Emily. Dan had never been in love before, but that day he could tell he felt something special.

After returning from vacation, Dan saw Emily at school, but it was not the same. She was popular, and it seemed everyone wanted to talk to her. Dan got frustrated; he couldn't understand why Emily had changed. He recalled when he enjoyed all of Emily's attention, now he couldn't get a decent two minutes. He took to posting pictures of them together on Snapchat to show his friends that Emily was more than a fantasy.

The photos Dan posted suggested an intimate relationship. When Emily found out about them, she asked him to take them down. That was the last straw for Dan and he posted one more picture. This one he was able to superimpose Emily's face on the body of a topless girl sunbathing. That's when the police got involved. Dan was accused of distributing child pornography. Dan lost Emily's friendship, the respect of his friends and gained the reputation of a sick weirdo.

Attention, affection and rejection are all equal in stirring our emotions. You must decide when to act (be aggressive) and when to let go. Affection that is not returned is a sign it is time to move on.

One day your heart will be broken. Those emotions and feelings will tear you apart and turn your world upside down. I can't begin to tell you how to get past this, but I will let you know that you will. Be strong, keep positive people near you and don't let this experience consume you. Time heals and as you meet other women, treat each relationship as a brand new one.

Learn from the past, don't repeat your mistakes, and learn to communicate openly and honestly. Before you pursue a woman, make sure you know yourself. That quality alone will make you more attractive than any tall, dark, handsome and confused man.

A woman needs a whole man. I will not court disaster by trying to tell you what a woman wants, but I can tell you what she needs and that's a whole man. A whole man has three distinct parts that tie together as one: Mind (soul), body and spirit. Our well-being comes from strengthening our mental health, physical health and spiritual health. Mentally we grow when we accomplish goals, overcome challenges and enjoy life's joyous moments. Physically we exercise our muscles, increase our stamina and push our limits. Spiritually we endure hardships, loss of close family members or friends, and accept the highest calling on our life for an eternal existence. This whole man takes time to develop. Be aware of who you are before you embark on unifying yourself with someone else.

Relationships take two people. Both willing to do whatever is necessary to keep it healthy and help it grow. If you are not a whole man a woman can't complete you. Two whole people come together and become one under God. So how do you know you've found the right other person? Ask God.

Before I go any further, we need to get one thing clear. There is a difference between love and lust. Both may attract but only one will last. I'll make it clearer; too many people start a physical relationship before they develop a friendship. Having sex just because you can has directed many for a trip on the broken relationship loop.

Let's look at the other side, some people have friends for life. They keep in contact with the same person for years; they meet on anniversaries, reach out on birthdays, call on holidays and involve themselves in the lives of friends' relatives for the sake of friendship.

This is the same type of relationship you should think of when you choose your mate. Do you make her laugh? Is she happy with you doing just about anything? What is it you love about this person? What is it you hate? How do you resolve problems? What makes her special? Why do you think she will be a life-long friend?

Friendships are based on trust, honesty and mutual respect. When you combine lust and sex in this decision, you confuse the friendship bond and link your emotions to sex. What happens when sex is not enough? What happens when you can't talk without arguing, the laughter and fun times are gone and all you have left is a person you don't know anymore, don't like and don't have anything in common with? What happens when there is no sex and that was the only thing keeping you in the relationship?

When I started this section, I talked about being a whole man. What I meant is you need to know yourself. What makes you happy, sad, excited, anxious, serious and stupid.

Know her too; know her enough to know you can make her happy. Of course, when you get married, you're making a promise to try to do just that.

One of the biggest keys to developing strong relationships is listening. Friends listen to each other. As you get older, you'll discover how having a friend that listens to you lifts your spirits and affirms you. You both need affirmation. When you pray with her include those things that she is having problems with and give them to God. Knowing that you are including her hopes and fears in your prayer to God solidifies your position as "Spiritual Head of the Household." Trust God, love large, but start by being a whole man.

Wisdom Tip

Find your heart in her eyes

BOTTOM LINE – Develop a lasting friendship first. Without friendship, love will not last. With friendship, love will last forever. Being friends first allows you to hear God when he moves your heart to commit to a lifetime.

BLESSING - 1 Peter 3:7 (NKJV)

Husbands, likewise, dwell with *them* with understanding, giving honor to the wife, as to the weaker vessel, and as *being* heirs together of the grace of life, that your prayers may not be hindered.

Hard work is eighth   *Colossians 3:23*

Mike liked his job. He liked being self-managed in that he could set his pace just as long as he made his quota, which he did again and again, consistently.

There were four people on the airplane chair repair detail. Mike, Pedro, Alex, and of course Arthur all worked on the same team, but separately. Pedro and Alex had been there the longest and had the most experience. Arthur had been picked up six months after Mike hired in. Arthur was quick, but he wasn't as detail orientated as the rest of the guys. Arthur wasn't organized either. He would misplace things and always had to borrow tools. Mike started not liking him when he would continue to ask to borrow his Snap-on ratchet. The ratchet was the one and only thing Mike had bought from the Snap-on truck that visited the shop monthly. It was his professional wrench, and Pedro had showed him how to personize it with an etching tool. Mike placed his initials on the large end between the Snap-on logo. He was smooth and after he finished it looked good, like they belonged there. Pedro said he should also place his initials or a mark one more place, where no one would think to look. Mike placed an M in the non-slip groves where your hand would be. Pedro was right, it blended in and Mike went to work.

Mike liked the mornings. He liked to get a cup a coffee and get started. There was a warehouse full of chairs to repair, and he liked taking them apart and putting them back together. When he finished everything worked flawlessly from semi-reclining to pulling out the trays. He did a good job, and he knew it.

On the last day, before vacation, Mike felt light and breezy. He was at work, but his mind was out at the beach. Then Author came into his workspace and asked to borrow his ratchet. Mike fell into reality, told Author a firm "no" and yelled for him to buy his own from the Snap-on truck that came every month. Arthur caught an attitude.

Mike didn't care. He was going on his first vacation with pay and his thoughts were on watching babes at the beach. Something about planning it on his own and using his own money to pay for it made it seem more special because he earned it. He felt this feeling of accomplishment as he locked his tools in his locker and left 30 minutes early for a one-week excursion in a seaside hotel on a semi-private beach. He had already packed and as he walked to his luggage loaded car, he grinned and whistled as he walked out the door. He had never felt so proud, so accomplished, so happy about himself. He was thinking a thought and as he sat down in the driver's seat the words came out, "This is Heaven."

Vacation is Over

Mike drove himself to work early the Monday morning following his vacation. His skin was drunk from sunbathing and though he had only been gone a week, he felt refreshed

Warren McDowell

and ready to get back to the job. He entered the shop and tasted the metallic air ripe with the scent of freshly brewed coffee. He was drawn to the coffee, but first things first. He knew he chucked his tools in their box in a rush and now he wanted to clean and oil them.

Mike went to his locker and when he touched the padlock it fell open. He thought nothing at first, everything seemed to be in order. He took out his tool box and sat it down on the bench. He then grabbed about five shop rags and a cup of black coffee before returning to the bench to indulge himself simmering the moment before everything comes to life. He begins to sing his favorite line from "The Wiz", the musical version of "Wizard of Oz". It's when Dorothy encourages the lion. Mike begins slow, but promises a strong finish. "I'm standing strong and tall. I'm the bravest of them all. If on courage, I must call, then I'll keep on trying and trying and trying. I'm a lion, in my own way, I'm a lion, a lion, a lion". As Mike goes through his toolbox, he knows something is not right, something is missing. He tries to retrace his actions the day he left, if he did anything stupid, and he was sure he didn't. As he frantically does a tool inventory, it becomes quite clear what it is. He doesn't see his Snap-on ratchet.

Back from vacation, early to work and feeling incomplete he knew what to do. He would wait till Arthur showed up. Mike had time to think and decided he wouldn't make a scene. He wouldn't mention his lock falling apart when he touched it. He would wait till everyone went to their workstations, then he would calmly go to Arthur and ask him for his wrench.

Things got started just like any other day. Everyone was there at 8 a.m. Job assignments where distributed and everyone welcomed Mike back except Arthur. He kept his distance and murmured a faint, "What's up." After they settled in their work areas, Mike knew it was time.

"Arthur, I can't find my Snap-on socket wrench, do you have it?" Mike asked.

"I don't know what you're talking about," replied Arthur.

Mike explained, "The socket wrench you liked to borrow is gone, do you have it?"

Arthur started getting loud, "I told you, I don't know what you're talking about."

Mike was furious, he tried to be calm, but he felt the anger seething inside, climbing up from his gut, making his heart race and speech slur. Before he could think he grabs Arthur's toolbox and empties everything out on the floor. Other employees began to gather to find out what is going on. Mike continues on as sees a ratchet.

Arthur screams, "Man, I don't have your racket. All I have are my tools, and you come here acting like a crazy. I'd take you out right now if it wasn't for all these people looking. The sun must have scorched your brain acting a fool like this."

Mike saw the ratchet and picked it up. Arthur said, "That's my ratchet, it's got my name on it, fool!"

Warren McDowell

Mike looked at the Snap-on ratchet, it looked like someone had run it through a meat grinder. It had grind marks all on it, and sure enough Arthur's name was ground in the handle. Inside the oval where Mike had artistically etched his initials, there was only rough defaced metal scaring the polished oval end where Mike initials were so painstakingly placed.

Mike looked at the defaced ratchet in awe. He couldn't believe someone would take the time to hide his ownership by cosmetically destroying a tool. Then he remembered the hidden M at the bottom on the handle. It blended in with the non-slip grooves and was almost impossible to see. He turned the ratchet bottom up and heard Arthur yell, "Put the wrench down fool."

That was the last thing he heard. It took four people to pull Mike off of Arthur. Although they found out what happened, management had strict rules about fighting on property. They also did not tolerate stealing. Based on the circumstances both men lost their jobs that day.

Every man is intended to work for a living. We are told to choose a career, point ourselves in that direction, work hard and we'll succeed. Some of us believe in and look to the easy life. Now here's the question, "What's the easy life, and how do I get it?". Nobody, I mean nobody wants life to be hard, difficult, tiring, brutal, unrewarding or unforgiving. We all want the "easy life."

So, we believe the lies that we just need to do enough to get by, we get paid to work not think, or ironically, we should work smarter not harder. We are so confused when the answer is easy, "Hard work keeps us alive and healthy."

My father worked two jobs most of his life. When he retired, he sat around on the back of his truck mostly talking with the other men who had retired in the neighborhood. He often spent most of his days at the house. He died not long after he retired, and I was shocked. Working every day myself, I still believed that finally we would have time to do things together, to become closer to talk about things we missed while he was working.

Months later, I realized that we can't sit around and do nothing or focus on leisure as a way of life. We are purposely designed with gifts, talents, hopes and dreams. If we are not living on purpose, then does death lure us with vain pursuits? The will to live comes at a cost; the desire to accomplish something.

Working not only satisfies that desire but gives us an outlet to exercise our gifts. When we pair our gifts and talents with a job we like, we find joy and possibly a successful career. Work is not a chore, it becomes life-giving energy.

One of my gifts includes problem solving. I can methodically define a process, isolate the problem by the process of elimination, find the cause, and then offer best-case solutions to resolve it. You may have a gift for relating to people and find yourself doing well in a sales or management position. You may like working with your hands and build custom tables and chairs. Working with animals, caring for others, being fascinated with numbers, electricity, the way things work, running faster than everyone else or basking in the applause from a stage performance, are just some of the areas you should attempt to celebrate life.

Then there are the traps, the distractions and obstacles that find ways to make our jobs difficult. They play on our weaknesses. Mike had a violent temper. Instead of going to his manager, he decided to handle the situation himself. Know yourself well enough to get help in your area of weakness. The outcome will be a lot brighter when we ask for help in a difficult situation instead of letting our weaknesses take control.

It takes time and experience to understand your talents as well as your weaknesses and realize what you've been born to do. Don't be afraid of new challenges that test your limits. That's the only way you grow to learn more about yourself.

> Wisdom Tip
>
> You can always tell how much someone wants something by what they give up to get it.

BOTTOM LINE –The things you value the most don't come easy.

BLESSING - Proverbs 14:23 (NIV)

All hard work brings a profit, but mere talk leads only to poverty

Ricky loved to bet. Most of all he loved to bet on himself. In high school the only time he caused trouble was when someone would bet him to do something they wouldn't do – like the time he walked through the girls' locker room naked. He collected $50 dollars and a three-day stay at home. His mother was hopping mad. His dad didn't matter; he only met him three times, when he was a baby. Ricky was his own man now. He gives his momma half his money and used the other half to treat himself like a king at Mickey D's, Jack in the Box or Home of the Whopper.

Those were the good ole days. His school days are over and Ricky works at a hardware store in the paint department. He has an eye for color and when someone brings in a color sample, he is the one who can blend the right colors of paint to match.

One of the Ricky's gifts is ability to tell what wet paint would look like when dry. Ricky is good at paint matching. So good that his fellow employees learned early that they would lose their money if they bet against Ricky matching a paint color. He loved to compete. As a little boy, he would race go carts but as he grew up, he decided to only bet on sure things. He didn't like things he couldn't control, so he started betting on himself, mastering a craft to get better. His mom would tell him that God had big plans for his life, and he only won because God's favor was upon his life. Ricky saw life as a competition, and he wasn't afraid of hard work. He went through paint training and spent time, his own time, blending till he matched the target color over and over again. He was good not because he guessed, but because he knew. He knew how red, yellow, and blue worked, how to lighten, how to soften, make it gloss, sparkle, shine or stay flat and finally what paint looked like when it dried.

Today was a Friday and a big day for him. It wasn't everyday someone turned 21. He started to count his blessings: from starting work at a hardware store part-time at sixteen to becoming part of the paint department and being selected for the training program that made him a paint mix master. Ricky knew he was special because a lot of his high school friends didn't make it out of high school. They either dropped out or went to jail. In a way the hardware store saved him, because he liked getting paid and they liked the way he worked.

This evening, his team from work planned to go to a nearby bar that announced a three-for-one special on shots. He would join them to celebrate his newly won right of being able to now legally drink alcohol in Texas. Ricky smiled. He had his own apartment, his own car, he was totally independent and now the beers in his fridge were legal.

The workday seemed to drift by in shifts, slow, fast, then extreme, as the weekend warriors readied themselves to make the most of home rehab projects. Happy hour was from 5 to 7 and as soon as 5 o'clock hit, Ricky hit the door. Karla and Jodi, accounting and personnel, got off at 4:30 and had already claimed a table. When Max, shipping & receiving, got there it was time to toast. That's when things started getting crazy. Max and Ricky got into a drinking contest and Ricky wouldn't back down. He claimed he could drink more than Max who was definitely a seasoned alcoholic. Max knew his limit and when Ricky put a 20 on the line for finishing three shots of tequila, Max knew it had to stop. Ricky, the birthday boy had won boasting rights for drinking everyone under the table, and he felt great. The adrenaline from winning always gave him a high and this time it was heightened because of the alcohol. Ricky told everyone he was going to the bathroom, but instead pushed through the crowd and went to his car. He was totally drunk and like Dorothy from the "Wizard of Oz" wanted nothing more than to click his heels three times and go home. That's all he remembered until he woke up at daybreak in his car on the highway shoulder facing the wrong direction.

As he backed his car up and made a U-turn, he prayed and thanked God for his protection. He knew he loved to compete, but now he knew that everything in life is not a competition. He put his car on the right side of the road and realized one other thing: "God is in control."

We compete daily. How and why we compete demands an answer. Some people will do almost anything to win. They view the win as the ultimate prize and develop a "win at all costs" type attitude in which they place themselves above everyone and everything. They become their own God, and that is one of the scariest and loneliest places to be.

As a teen, you mainly compete against the guy next door, your schoolmates and your classmates. Then your competition expands into a larger world as you look for a job with rivals that include college graduates and other skilled workers. Now, with the technological advances in communication, we compete locally and abroad, finding ourselves head to head with people in other counties managing projects, balancing budgets, supporting products, services or creating sales materials.

When, how, and why we compete chisels our character and forms the foundation of what we are. From the football field, to the science fair, from the cook-off to the talent show, our world presents competition as a way of life. The ones who win are not randomly selected. They have spent the time it takes to prepare for the challenges, and that is what you must do. Once you find your passion, take the time to develop yourself in this competing world.

My dad always said, "if you're going to be something, be the best." In my field, we have SMEs, which stands for Subject Matter Experts. He or she has trained or studied enough to be the go-to person for answers to problems in their field. There is great value in being an SME. When workforce reductions occur, the SME is often still in demand and remains. Being the best in your field helps guarantee employment. But it's not just something you say about yourself. It takes desire and hard work to have people acknowledge you as an expert in your field based solely on the work you do.

```
                    Wisdom Tip

             The hardest part of winning
           is accepting the sacrifice it takes
```

BOTTOM LINE – Winning is only important when you're in the right race.

BLESSING – 2 Timothy 2:5 (NKJV)

And also if anyone competes in athletics, he is not crowned unless he competes according to the rules.

Opportunity is Yours   *Galatians 6:9-10*

Gene was going into the army. He had scored high on an abilities assessment, attacking the test where each assortment of questions made him weary. His resolve was clear: finish what you start and be thankful for the challenges in life that make you strong.

Gene had his life planned. He grew up in a multiracial family where his father spoke French and his mother Spanish. Though he could speak a little of both languages, Gene was focused on computers as the wave of the future. He would study Information Technology (IT). He planned a career in IT support that can be performed anywhere, then find a tropical place after the army to settle down. He never expected the recruiter to tell him that the abilities assessment has revealed his talent for foreign languages and encourage him to change his major course of study to French and Chinese.

Gene was furious; if the army wanted him, they should honor his wishes. This was similar to the kind of bait and switch tactics stores use when they advertise an item just to get people into the store then try to sell them a similar item at a higher price. Even though Gene was talented in foreign languages, he was determined to stick to his plan. He wanted training in the Information Technology field and that was that; nothing more, nothing less. He stuck to his guns and held his ground.

Even when they showed him his talent assessment, his income potential and his future job assignment, Gene wouldn't budge. He refused to see and finally got what he wanted. He was satisfied. He had fought a war about his planned future and was able to come out on top.

The three years he spent in the army were invaluable. He learned about communication networks. It was when he got his first corporate job that he began to understand that today's networks are world connecting and if he could communicate in different languages, he could expand his role as part of the North American team to become a global player. His boss didn't have Gene's experience or knowledge in connecting networks, but he spoke four languages and flew all over the world.

Throughout life, we are given lots of choices. Every day presents us with opportunities to rise or sink. When experiencing these pivotal moments, we need to seek God's answer for our lives through prayer and ask for His direction.

My wife and I built a house. We took on the role as general contractor and interviewed all the contractors from the concrete foundation constructor, plumber, electrician, framer, sheetrocker, tile setter, wood floor layer and painter. Some contractor choices were clear, but the framer – the person that takes the wood and builds the frame of the house – was not clear. We had three different people from whom to choose with different estimates on what they would charge. We were stuck, so we prayed that God would give us the answer and He did. The cell phones of two of the contractors stopped working. We wrote a contract with Mario and had a great frame, trim work and siding done through him. We know the frame is excellent. It's been inspected three times.

Other contractors we chose did not work out as well. Our plumber quit on us and we had to fire the painter. Had we asked God his choice in these other two trades, things would have been a lot better. We thought we knew what was best for building our future home just like Gene thought he knew what was best for his future. There is a quote by clergyman Ben Herbster that says, "The biggest waste is the difference between who we are and who we could be." Each of us has unique talents that need to be recognized, embraced and developed. They are the keys to unlock our destiny. There are always challenges and opportunities waiting for us, and our acceptance or rejection shapes our lives and molds our soul.

There were times in my life when I was frustrated with my job. My co-workers were leaving, being hired by other companies and the job market was hot. I had a really great resume. I put it online, but I got no hits, no emails, no phones calls, no notice at all. Two people with less experience went on to higher paying jobs, and I couldn't understand it. Then the tragic events of 9/11 happened and those people who had left were the ones who were being let go from their new jobs. Projects were being canceled and company growth postponed. I was right where I should be. God knew I was frustrated to the point that if any opportunity came up I would have taken it just to get out and He closed that door for me. Now I pray that God opens doors that are right and closes those that are wrong.

When I trust in God, I don't have to worry, because He chooses my direction. You have that same opportunity right now. The stories here were told to help you see how much we are alike and how the choices we make, make us.

Don't be afraid of challenges and position yourself where God can accelerate your growth. That may be by writing a book, starting your own business or learning a new job. Like Solomon, ask God for wisdom and He will direct your path. You have the opportunity to work with less stress and more happiness, but it requires you to trust God and commit.

Committing to something means facing the fear of the unknown because you know you have to. Commit includes two parts: plan and action. Once you commit to a desired future state, you have to plan and act to reach your goal. If you commit to a fight, you have to develop a power move, know how to strike, when to dodge, and finally, determine the best time and place to confront your enemy.

Men rarely commit to anything unless we believe we can win. For a boy to commit to an uncertain future is almost impossible. It takes confidence in knowing yourself: having a realistic idea about what you can accomplish by doing it enough times to know the result. Then trust yourself

Warren McDowell

enough to try new things, forge new paths, climb new mountains, reach new goals. Committing to something brings you to the fight.

Yes it is a fight.

You fight to avoid letting the crowd lead you and stay true to your purpose.

You fight to reach your goals and keep your integrity.

You fight to protect your loved ones and create a safe place for them to grow.

You fight to remain flexible and find opportunity in an ever-changing world.

You fight to work your passion and grow it in areas that support your family financially.

You fight to keep romance alive and discover a new relationship with the same woman you married.

You fight to lead your family and assume your position as, "Spiritual head of the Household".

You fight to resist temptation and not do something stupid because you think no one will find out.

You fight to tear down walls of miscommunication and open doors when the truth is hidden.

You fight to control your anger and remain sensitive to the lives of those you touch.

You fight to help others when they need help in the fight.

You fight……..

James 1:12 Blessed is the man who perseveres under trial, because when he has stood the test, he will receive the crown of life that God has promised to those who love him.

Earlier I shared that as long as I can remember my father worked two jobs and soon after he retired, he died. He never got to meet my wife. He never got to talk to me about cherishing the good times in my marriage, so I can remember and hold them when the difficult times arrive. He never met my kids. He never had the chance to give me advice on motivating, disciplining or encouraging my children. We didn't have the conversations on child development or most importantly how to help a boy transition to a young man and eventually a man.

I know I was missing a lot, and I still am. I'm sharing with you what has helped me.

The thing is, I've heard this same story from different men of all nationalities. Men whose fathers were there and not. Men whose fathers retired and died, and lastly, men who had no father at all. I've learned we (men) have to work (Gen 3:19 and 2Thess 3:10). We have to keep busy doing something that provides and matters to us.

When we are not following God's plan, we become spiritually idle, lose ourselves to the world and follow the paths that empty us and can lead to death. My father died of a stroke in his bed. His face was one in which we knew he was at peace and with God. I want everyone to know that peace. I also want you to be spiritual warriors and accept your role as the "Spiritual head of the Household." You can do that.

This is a start. I hope your search for self includes finding out all you can about Jesus. The rest will happen. Be patient and learn to pray. Grab one of God's promises and hold on to it with all your heart. My personal favorite is John 15:7 "If you abide in Me, and My words abide in you, you will ask what you desire, and it shall be done for you." Let His words remain in you. Learn to quote Him and you'll discover the power of the spoken word that has no limits. With it you can accomplish anything: increase your love, increase your faith, bless others, move mountains, help people accept His love.

You have the opportunity to choose. You choose who you want to be. You choose...............your character, your goals, your life, your fight.

```
Wisdom Tip

Opportunity is always hidden
from those that don't try
```

BOTTOM LINE – Do your homework. It's the small steps that prepare us for the large leap through an open door

BLESSING – Proverbs 3:5-6 (NKJV)

Trust in the LORD with all your heart, and lean not on your own understanding; in all your ways acknowledge Him, and He shall direct your paths.

Back to the Beginning

Isn't it funny how we always manage to come back to the beginning? Who are you? Do you command the presence and respect of other men? Are you a taker? Are you still finding your way? Have you made plans for your future? Has the world discouraged you? Have you even started trying to put it together? Do you have a plan? Are you making it up as you go along? Do you know what your passion is? Do you feel empty? Do you believe you are missing something?

Your decisions determine your direction.

Your direction determines your destiny.

The fact that you have read this guide to helping you determine where you are in your journey is impressive. Now comes the time for action. One of my most favorite movies is "The Iron Giant." It's an animated story in which a giant war machine robot lands on earth. He is befriended by a little boy and taught our language. During the course of time, the robot learns that he likes to play the part of the hero. As he and the boy play together, they realize the robot can't stop his self-defense systems designed to attack when threatened. The army eventually finds out about the robot and attack him. The robot retreats, but when he believes the boy is dead, he goes into full combat mode destroying all who attack him until he sees the boy who reminds him that he can choose what he wants to be. The robot chooses to be a hero and saves the city from a nuclear attack. At the moment when the robot is about to intercept a missile aimed at the city, he recounts the words of his friend, "You choose who you want to be."

It's not easy determining what you believe about God. Will you establish whether you feed and grow your passion? Can you resolve the experiences that shape your character? Do you make decisions to plan to accomplish short, medium and long-term goals? Shall you chase after money or learn to maximize your wealth doing the things you love. Will you accept the roles of responsibility that come with a family? When you decide to share your heart with the love of your life, will you keep the lines of communication open and remember the key that unlocks her heart?

How do you make the right decisions? When do you unlock your man potential?

I talked to men about defining the moment when a boy turns into a man and found most of us believe that a boy becomes a man when he begins to make decisions on his own. Women say a boy becomes a man when he is able to support himself financially: pay his own way. The world says a boy becomes a man when he takes responsibility for his actions. I wrote earlier that a boy becomes a man when he dedicates his life to a purpose greater than himself.

I didn't believe these answers were entirely right or wrong. However, during the writing of this book, I've come to a different conclusion. What I've learned, – what my son has taught me - is the most important part of being a man is learning self-control. It is also one of the hardest lessons to learn. You can set your values, make your goals, plan your future, decide your path, determine your career, select your friends, even submit to our God, but if you haven't learned to control yourself, you will stumble.

The next hardest lesson is God control.

When I think about self-control, I am sincere about defining those things I will NOT do. I understand daily I have to choose my actions, think my words, calm my anger, let go my frustrations, seek a perfect solution, show an empathetic smile, or express brotherly love, and I know I can't do this without help.

Prayer is my call for help. Just like Carrie Underwood's song "Jesus Take the Wheel," you can submit to the creator and ask for His direction, intervention, deliverance.

You see, it is by gaining control of yourself you can abstain from your selfish desires and embrace the qualities of the Forever Loving Father God.

My family have been blessed enough to enjoy a one-week vacation at the beginning of fall. One year we went to a condo on the beach and my four daughters were really excited. One of them is a water baby which means from her earliest moments she loved playing in the water, from the tub to puddles in the driveway. We got settled in and went to check out the grounds. I didn't notice she had slipped on her bathing suit under her t-shirt and shorts.

She wasn't more than five years old and we knew she needed swimming lessons. Long story short, we came to the pool. We went into the gated pool area and you guessed it, as soon as we were poolside my daughter slips off her t-shirt, shorts and jumps in the deep end. She didn't notice it was the deep end until she went under and her feet didn't hit the ground. Being the natural water baby, she, just jumped. I was busy trying to survey just how comfortable the lawn chairs were going to be when I heard the half-choked call, "Dad!"

Don't know how I got there, but I overcame the chairs and was in the water holding her next to me. She coughed out the words, "Sorry, daddy." I cradled her in my arms and told her it was okay. After realizing my wallet and cell phone went in with me, I added, "but don't ever do that again."

Since then we have given our daughter swimming lessons. In fact, there is a class where she can learn how to save someone from drowning.

Here's the thing, when you are drowning in the world and you call out, God will hear your cry. His Son's life and words revealed in the Bible gives us swimming lessons. He will reach out, pull you close and save you.

Study His life, put His words in you and you will learn to swim the waters of a selfish, greedy, self-absorbed world. Better than that, you will learn how to teach others to

Warren McDowell

swim. Read the bible and discover for yourself how the words come to life.

This book – the Bible is a book about relationships. God's relationship to man, man's relationship to God and man's relationship to man (our relationship to each other). When a person expresses his faith (religious preference), you will hear one of two things: religion or relationship. When I hear a person talk about their religion, I turn a deaf ear. When I hear someone talk about their relationship, I know they know Him and that's what makes us His children. Daily, we swim with instructions from the greatest swim coach in the world.

Get in the living water, learn to swim, help others learn and save people's lives.

Wisdom Tip

My best moments were
spent helping others

BOTTOM LINE – the younger you are when you start reading the bible, the sooner you will find answers to being happy in everyday life.

BLESSING – Proverbs 3:13 (NKJV)

**Happy *is* the man *who* finds wisdom,
And the man *who* gains understanding**

I wish I could tell you more, but I wanted this book to be short and simple.

I have one more thing.

I love you son.

With all my heart and I want you to know that I always will.

I hate defining a word with the same word but this time I'm going to break that rule two times.

You see I've also learned, "Love, loves to love."

It is my prayer that as you grow, you will continue to listen, learn and love.

DAD

Warren McDowell

Father's Words of Wisdom

When I stated this project I sent out the following email below. I am honored by the responses and have included them for you. We all need to know what is expected of us and I believe the earlier the better. As you read these remember someday this will be you. What will you leave that will last forever?

> Jimmy,
>
> I am writing a book for young men and need your help.
>
> Could you please take the time and send me 20 things you would like your son to know if your time on this earth was limited to 2 weeks.
>
> That's it. I would really appreciate the input. May God continue to bless you and your family.
>
> Warren

The following pages are the thoughts and advice of fathers to their sons. Please read it knowing that they are talking to you.

Wisdom Tip

There are 31 Chapters in the book of Proverbs. Read Chpt 1 on first day of Month. Chpt 2 on day 2, 3 on day 3 everyday and you will complete the book. Repeat every month. Add this to your daily bible reading together with one chapter of old testament, one chapter new testament and a chapter in the book of Psalms

Warren McDowell

Bob Coffman's list

1. The Plan of Salvation - The importance of hearing and responding to the Gospel at the earliest age possible
2. The principle of *The Exchanged Life* - Following 1.) above, to learn the truths of Gal. 2:20 as a Christ follower (i.e. How to let Christ live His life in them moment-by-moment, by faith)
3. The importance of developing the habit of a daily Quiet Time (time in the Word and Prayer) in the morning to start each day
4. The importance of developing a Strong work ethic – To understand the value of a Dollar earned through; hard work, persistence, grit and integrity
5. To develop an Attitude of Gratitude in life – to take nothing for granted, to be thankful at all times
6. To wait on God's timing regarding the Spouse that He has lined up for him. God has a "perfect match" in store if we will wait on Him
7. The importance of being a man and just saying NO to drugs and premarital sex
8. The importance of finishing what you start in life: Schooling, Scouting, Work Commitments, Personal Commitments, etc.
9. The importance of knowing and following your personal "bent" (i.e. personality, talents, interests, etc.) and being all you can be in this area. Not everyone is meant to be an engineer, plumber, soldier, doctor, teacher but <u>all really enjoy their work</u> throughout their career when they follow this approach

10. That you love him deeply (more than he will ever know) and that he is and will be loved and accepted by his Mom and Dad at all times, NO MATTER WHAT

11. The importance of being the Godly Servant Leader and Protector of his family when he marries and has children

12. To learn to laugh often and enjoy life and to refuse to be one who is "serious at all times"

13. To learn to listen more and talk less (this is applicable for ALL ages)

14. To learn what it means to be a gentleman who is kind and considerate with the *"gentler sex"*

15. Assuming you are an American... To be patriotic, to love your country and be willing to defend her... (we are so blessed to be a part of this great land)

16. But, with respect to 15.) above assuming you are a Christian... To realize that we belong to God's Kingdom, owe Him our first allegiance and that we are "just passing through"...

17. To learn polite manners and how to show respect to women and the elderly

18. To understand that "success" is not measured by the size of one's bank account or one's position

19. To remember that his parents aren't as "dumb" or "clueless" as they may seem. They were once his age and they know more about "that issue" (whatever it is) than you realize...

20. To not blame God for taking me (as his Father) out of this world at such a young age and to remember that He has a Heavenly Father that <u>he can absolutely count on</u> the rest of his life

Warren McDowell

From: **FELDMAN, STEVE**

Advice to young men

No. 1 - Seek a real and personal relationship with Jesus Christ. It can be stronger and closer relationship than with your best friend or mother.

Read your Bible daily, and meditate on God's Word. Pray constantly.

Ask Jesus for wisdom and guidance daily; at work ask Him what you should be working on. Around co- workers, friends, relatives, ask Him how to deal with them.

Forgiveness is the key to your relationship with Him and all others. Treat all with respect; even those that you think don't deserve it.

Your heart is going to get broken at least once, remember your true, true love, Jesus; He is the only one that will never forsake you.

Avoid debt, except for a house but always put down at least 20% and pay it off quickly, less than 15 years. Everything else, pay cash, even a vehicle. Vehicles are very expensive, especially when considering how they lose their value. A $30k SUV is worth only $10k in 4 to 5 years.

When going thru tough times remember "THIS TOO WILL PASS" He will see you thru.

Luis Rengifo,

In no particular order:

1. Save 10% of your salary.
2. Put your happiness first. Do what makes you happy – money will follow.
3. Be the best you can be.
4. Be flexible / adaptable.
5. Respect different points of view.
6. Respect different nationalities, religions, backgrounds.
7. Find what you're really good at, and try to be the best at it.
8. When in conflict, try to find common ground. In most cases you will find that we have more in common than not.
9. Always try to lead by example. Learn the subject matter, and demonstrate to your team that you can do the job at hand.
10. Be a good listener; it's the best way to gain buy-in, even if in the end you make a different decision.
11. Try to rid yourself of pre-conceptions. You waste a lot of time reacting to people and situations based on your pre-conceptions.
12. Don't take on a partner who doesn't value or respect you.
13. Try to be as prepared as possible before you have kids of your own; they depend on you and look up to you – be the best you can be for them.
14. Work is important … but doesn't take precedence over you or your family.

15. Be self-sufficient. Don't depend on alcohol, drugs, food or other vices to be fulfilled.
16. Don't allow problems at home to affect your work, and vice-versa.
17. Exercise.
18. Visit the doctor, dentist and eye-doctor once per year.
19. Call your mom and dad at least once a week.
20. Have a hobby

From: Ruby, Jason

1. I love you very much
2. I am very proud of you
3. Always obey the (10) commandments
4. Always be ready to share Christ's love to everyone God puts into your life
5. You are a Godly young man; continue to trust & obey God all the days of your life
6. Please always have your quiet time with God each day before your day starts
7. With God's help you can accomplish your heart's desire if you are in the center of God's will
8. Always take your family to church
9. Be the spiritual leader of your family
10. Serve your wife and children
11. Always work unto the Lord at your job
12. Serve the Lord with the gifts He has given you
13. Love God with all your heart and soul
14. Love your wife and kids as God loves His children
15. Be a Godly man of integrity
16. Be in an accountability group with other Christian men
17. Always pick Godly friends
18. Always lead a Godly example to your family, colleagues, friends, and neighbors
19. Let God always lead and guide you in everything you do
20. I love you very much

From: **Akins, Allen**

1. Say what you mean and mean what you say
2. No matter how much money a man has, it his word is no good then he is no good
3. Always have pure intention
4. Always be honest
5. Look a person in the eyes when you talk with them
6. Be quick to listen and slow to speak
7. Enjoy every breath
8. Never worry because worrying solves nothing
9. Looking bad is a derivative of low self esteem
10. Love your neighbor…your neighbor is the person you are next to at that moment
11. Take 5 seconds before you answer any question to make sure you are thinking before you are speaking
12. Once you are married, all marriage escape doors should be bolted shut, with a 5 inch metal plate in front of it
13. Your children should see you experiencing every emotion out there to know how to control it and not le the emotion control you
14. Treat your wife so good that every woman who knows her or see you two together should envy her for having you
15. You can make your wife to the exact way you want by encouraging her and motivating her to the things you like and praying that God work out the things on the inside.
16. Learn to cook and clean so you are not dependent on any woman

17. Do nice things for people not because you looking for a reward but because it is the right thing to do
18. Learn and practice the laws of sowing and reaping
19. Speaking to people never hurt anyone nor does it cost anything....therefore say hi to people as you walk by
20. Trust in God the father, God the Son, and God the Holy Spirit ALWAYS!!

From: **Toy Leach**

1. You have to have a relationship with Jesus to make it to heaven.
2. Take care of our Family Your (Mom needs your attention)
3. Let your Yes be Yes and your No be No.
4. You have to love your neighbor as yourself
5. Be strong in the Lord.
6. Stand firm in your faith
7. Fight temptation like it's a sickness that is life threatening.
8. Walk and be led by the spirit
9. Do not let a day go by without sowing seed. (love, joy, peace and money)
10. Always give your money to who God tells you too. Keep your money clip loaded.
11. Don't let your pride steal someone's blessing
12. Be a cheerful giver.
13. Do everything to your best ability
14. A female can make you or brake you. Let a Godly one make you the Man God wants you to be...!!!
15. Have nothing to prove
16. Have nothing to hide
17. Have nothing to fear
18. Be yourself! The way God Made you
19. Keep your eyes open
20. Live life, don't settle for average

From: **Moore, Tim**

1. Read your Bible every day. Read Proverbs every day. There are 31 Proverbs; read the Proverb that corresponds with the day of the month to keep you on track. Reading Proverbs everyday is the number one recommendation that I can give to living a worthwhile life with no regrets.

2. Making a lot of money does not matter. I don't think there has ever been someone on his death bed who said "I regret that I did not make another million dollars", but I do know there have been many people who regret not spending more time with their kids and working on relationships.

3. The Bible can be trusted as reliable and true; read it and believe it.

4. Don't trust what the World expects from you, refer back to #3

5. Don't let me or anybody else determine what you should do with your life. You know what your calling is; go for it. If you need advice, fine, ask away. But again, if you know your calling, don't let anyone talk you out of it.

6. Make sure you do not let anyone drag your character down. You will become more like the people you hang around the most. Hang around the right people.

7. Do whatever it takes to keep your pecker in your pants; wait until you are married. The psychological and emotional damage I've seen in others who could not or refused to wait is great. Refer back to number

8. Get to know Jesus more and more and tell others about Him and what He has done for you.
9. Nothing has destroyed the families and lives of your relatives than alcohol. Stay away from it; it is not in your genes to play around with it.
10. If you have done something wrong, confess it immediately to God and seek reconciliation from others as soon as possible when applicable.
11. Tithe. You are much better off living with 90% of your income with God than 100% without Him. His help and guidance from trusting him is rewarding. I can confess that I have learned this lesson the hard way and this has been a struggle for me. Finances are one area that God says to put him to the test on; trust Him on this.
12. Life is hard for everyone – rich and poor alike. Respect everyone and never ever make fun of anyone. God created everyone; if you make fun of someone, then consider yourself making fun of God.
13. When you go on a date with a girl, remember that she is someone's daughter
14. Always be as honest as you possibly can. Don't be afraid to say "I don't know".
15. Treat others as you want to be treated – the true Golden Rule and don't forget rule number 12.

Mike Vaughn

To my son on life

God

Remain humble in good times and bad. God resists the proud.
Seek God's perspective on everything. Do what he says.

Family

Demonstrate selfless devotion.
Be a good listener.
Live your sermon instead of preaching it.
Watch for something praiseworthy and praise out loud.

Character

Work harder on yourself, than you do on your job.
Keep your promises no matter what it costs you.

Passion

Passion comes from knowing your purpose and pursuing it daily.

Goals

Success is the progressive realization of a worthwhile dream. The most worthwhile dream is the one God has for your life.
A goal is not a goal until it is written down and read daily.

Money

God owns everything. I own nothing.
Don't pursue things, pursue the One who owns everything.
Give 1st – at least 10% / Save 2nd – at least 10% / Spend last – no debt
Always remember, God is your source.

Women

Be a lifelong student of your wife.
Pray with your wife and for your wife (out loud) everyday.
Give your wife at least one 60 second hug per day.

Hard work

You will be compensated in direct proportion to the number of people you are serving and the quality of your service.
Measure success in the number of people whose lives you are impacting for the good.

Competition

Leaders create, they don't compete.

Opportunity

The crossroad of life is where opportunity and preparedness meet.
Most opportunities come cleverly disguised as a problem that needs solving.

20 saying for my sons: -   **Kevin Stewart**

1. Have the fortitude and principles to protect and fight for that that you believe in. Be your own man and make your own informed decisions.
2. Admit that we all are sinners as the Bible says and receive Jesus Christ in the salvation of your soul. Listen to God's Holy Spirit in you to battle/control the sinful flesh-pleasing spirit within.
3. Follow the 10 Commandments of God to the best of your abilities. Stay to Christian values as defined by God's word even/especially if it takes you against those who choose not to.
4. Honor your word and be careful that you can do so before giving it.
5. Keep a positive attitude and let joy be in your spirit. Develop a spirit of humility, and be thankful in everything.
6. Make legitimate money in an honorable profession/career that you naturally love and invest education and hard work into it.
7. Live to the level that you can afford; Take reasonable financial chances on good/safe opportunities that will help you achieve success.
8. Do not assume that all non-African American people are out to get you based on your race; yet, discern and avoid those who are.
9. Keep self control and think through all situations; do not act on your feeling in the sensitive or less than ideal situations that you will find yourself in at times.
10. Be careful with who you attach yourself to as a friend. Long-term associations bring about simulation.

11. Treat women with respect and avoid those that do not deserve it.
12. Marry a woman that truly loves you. Have children and develop a good fatherly relationship with them. Show hugging affections toward them and parent them is a spirit of love.
13. Be responsible to living a Bible-based life style in front of your wife and children. Lead them to knowing Christ and God's word for themselves. Raise them in a Bible-based Church that teaches and preaches God's Word. Tithe and serve in that church yourself.
14. Balance your work life and family life to be able to enjoy both. Spend quality time with your family.
15. Do not get into to much debt and work to pay it off as soon as possible.
16. Know when to back out of and stop the uncontrollable/ wrong things that give you stress. Change/correct them if you can.
17. Take care of your body and avoid things that will damage it short and long term. Do not smoke anything, nor drink yourself out of control. Stay away from drugs of all kind and limit prescribed pills.
18. Do not give yourself to the temporary pleasures that will cost you later. Avoid ill-advised sexual pleasures and admit that 'Abstinence is better'.
19. Forgive yourself when you make a mistake and own up to it to correct it.
20. Promote only the good in all people and avoid despising or harboring hate for anyone in your heart. Show forgiveness and mercy when you are lead to.

From: **Tony Simmons**

God

None of us knows the absolute truth. Allow yourself to question your beliefs. Ask why you believe and seek the truth. Just because you were raised to believe something does not make it right. Seek God, not religion. Religion is man-made. You can find God in the woods at least as easily in the woods or by the ocean as you can in a building.

Money

Put your money in savings like any other bill. Pay your bills first before you play. Don't spend what you don't have. Live smaller and play more. Live in the smallest place, drive the cheapest car. Pack your lunch for work.

Family

Love your family. Take care of your health so you can provide for them. Be a good example.

Women

Don't sleep around. The fewer the number of women you have sex with, the easier it is to be pleased. Don't watch porn. It's unrealistic. You're probably not built like those men. Don't expect your wife to act like those women.

Character

Be good. Let your word be your bond. Be worthy of respect. Treat others the way you want to be treated and give them a reason to treat you that way.

Hard Work

Find something you love to do and put your heart into it. Work will be easier that way. Work hard when you have to, but at the end of the day, work smarter not harder. Develop a habit of hard work, especially in your yard and in the gym. You'll appreciate that when you're my age and have a strong healthy body.

Passion

Find your passion and pursue it. If you can parlay your passion into a career, you'll do very well.

Competition

Don't be consumed with competition with anyone but yourself. You don't have to beat anyone. We can all win. Let the good in you nurture the good in others.

Goals

Set lofty goals and pursue them. Also set little goals along the way. Reward yourself with self praise. Be ambitious.

Opportunity

Because my nature is to be the hero and inject myself into dangerous situations, I've tried to teach my son everything I've thought he needed to know. Here are just some random thoughts that I've tried to teach.

We who are strong have a moral obligation to protect the week. Take some self defense classes so that you can physically protect others if you have to. Women love a man who makes them feel safe.

Eat healthy. Again, you'll appreciate the good habits when your metabolism slows down when you're older.

Read the encyclopedia, the dictionary, and the thesaurus instead of watching TV. Read about science, history, and math. Find something and make yourself an expert. You are responsible for your own education, not your school, not your job. Learn trivia. Learn as much as you can about everything. It makes you interesting.

Learn to tell good jokes. People love to laugh, and they love a man who makes them laugh.

Everyone is faulty. Everyone is in the same boat as you are, so you're as good as anyone. NOBODY IS BETTER THAN YOU ARE!!!! Show respect, but remember you are also worthy of respect. If you honestly don't think you are, change your life for the positive.

Be the man you want the world to think you are. Live that way even in private when nobody is around.

From: **Buelle Hill**

#1. Trust God in all you do
#2. Family 2nd behind God
#3. Be kind to each other
#4. Have respect for yourself as well as others
#5. Don't sweat the small stuff - in the end it will all work out one way or the other
#6. Take time for yourself
#7. Whistle while you work
#8. Work hard, play hard, love with passion
#9. Be true to yourself
#10. Don't worry ~ lift it up to a higher power
#11. Be Happy
#12. Tell the truth even when it hurts
#13. Help those in need that can't help themselves
#14. Have mercy and forgiving even when you are wronged or hurt
#15. Try to find the good in people instead of the bad
#16. Stay positive
#17. Stay focused on the Big picture
#18. Be Thankful/Grateful
#19. If it's worth doing, it's worth doing right
#20. Always leave a place better than it was when you arrived

From: **David Brown**

1. You can eat a Volkswagen if you cut it into small enough pieces. Cut your problems down into small enough sizes so that you can easily understand them and solve them. Once solved, move on to the next piece until you have dispatched the entire turd.
2. Be aware of your environment. Many problems are caused by a lack of situational awareness and can be easily avoided by merely paying attention to what is going on in your immediate vicinity.
3. You are a good man, but the woods IS full of 'em! (from my father)
4. You only have one mother. Always, I mean ALWAYS treat her with respect and reverence.
5. You are unique and special. There is no one out there like you with your unique personality, abilities and deficits.
6. Shoot for the stars and you might hit the ceiling fan
7. It's never over until you give up
8. Try not to lead with your chin unless it's a sure thing
9. There are no sure things in life
10. Anger, pain and resentment have energy. You cannot destroy energy only change its form. Emotional energy must be dealt with in a healthy manner or it will cause physical and mental damage. Healthy ways to deal with emotional energy: Exercise, music, writing, reading, art, etc. Unhealthy ways: Alcohol, drugs, sex, cruelty, etc.

11. Your heart is where your money is. Show me where you spend your money and I'll show you where your heart is.
12. Abortion is murdering another human being. Don't do it.
13. If your gut tells you something is wrong, it probably is
14. Temptation will flee from you if you just say no
15. Seek to have a pure heart if you want to find God.
16. What is God? God is Truth, Light and Love.
17. What is love?
18. The penis does not have a brain or a conscience
19. The mind is its own worst deceiver. Know thyself.
20. You can learn almost anything if you practice it enough
21. What God is, has very little to do with what people do as they practice their man-made religions. Try to discover the difference between God and man-made religion. Don't get the two confused.
22. Data about data is not data.
23. You will make many mistakes and many bad things will happen to you. Try to roll with the punches and don't let it get you down. Your most valuable asset is your self esteem, try to keep the weeds out of your self esteem garden and you will be happy. Seek always to do those things that will accrue to your self esteem positively.
24. You can be much more productive if you are not concerned with who gets the credit
25. When good things happen, realize that you are not totally responsible
26. When bad things happen, first take total personal responsibility for everything as a starting point.

Don't blame others even if some of it is their fault. Ask yourself what could you have done differently to have prevented this; then work your way out from there so you can clearly understand the root cause and eventually solve this problem or avoid future problems. Try to learn from mistakes.

27. There is no success that can compensate for failure in the home

28. Intelligence is the glory of God

29. No is an answer and sometimes THE answer. Also, no answer is an answer. Think about it.

30. Beware of your government. Stay up with current events and know your history

31. The government is not your friend and has its own selfish agenda

32. Don't believe gossip

33. Don't believe everything you read or hear. Go to the source and discover the truth for yourself.

34. Everyone has an agenda

35. Be "cause" over effect, not the effect of someone else's cause

36. Complete cycles. Don't do anything half-ass, complete the entire process and then move on to the next.

37. Moderation is the key

38. An important difference between a winner and a loser is that the winner has usually failed many more times than the loser.

39. Humility and thankfulness are precursors to happiness

40. Always treat women with reverence and respect. The benefits of this will reap vast rewards to you, your wife and your family.

At the beginning of this book was a
condensed statement about Purpose

from David Viscott. Below is the original quote.

The purpose of life is to discover your gift.
The work of life is to develop it.
The meaning of life is to give your gift away.

The question was asked: What is your gift?

My answer:
The LOVE that is more powerful than life itself.
Freely given by the Lord's son